SAURABH KATIYAR

THE AWAKENING
AND BREAKING THE SELF ILLUSION

BLUEROSE PUBLISHERS
India | U.K.

Copyright © Saurabh Katiyar 2025

All rights reserved by author. No part of this publication may be reproduced, stored in a retrieval system or transmitted in any form or by any means, electronic, mechanical, photocopying, recording or otherwise, without the prior permission of the author. Although every precaution has been taken to verify the accuracy of the information contained herein, the publisher assume no responsibility for any errors or omissions. No liability is assumed for damages that may result from the use of information contained within.

BlueRose Publishers takes no responsibility for any damages, losses, or liabilities that may arise from the use or misuse of the information, products, or services provided in this publication.

For permissions requests or inquiries regarding this publication, please contact:

BLUEROSE PUBLISHERS
www.BlueRoseONE.com
info@bluerosepublishers.com
+91 8882 898 898
+4407342408967

ISBN: 978-93-7018-727-6

Cover design: Daksh
Typesetting: Tanya Raj Upadhyay

First Edition: April 2025

Preface

I was born free. So were you.

No name, no caste, no religion. Just an unshaped soul — infinite, fearless, and untamed.

But the world doesn't like free minds.

They gave me a name, and suddenly I was someone — but someone by their definition, not mine. They stamped me with an identity before I could even speak. They built a cage around my mind and called it "education." They measured my worth with grades, told me obedience was wisdom, and warned me that stepping off the path meant ruin.

They convinced me — and you — that success is a title, a job, or a number in a bank account. They told us freedom means fitting in, being accepted, and staying quiet. They called it life. But it's **slavery** — wrapped in gold, disguised as a dream.

This book is not a gentle hand or a motivational pat on the back. **This book is a weapon.**

It's a sword to cut through the lies and burn down the illusions. It's a mirror, forcing you to look at the version of yourself you were never meant to become — the one shaped by fear, greed, and conformity.

You were never meant to be a follower. You were never meant to live a life someone else designed for you.

The world told you to chase success. I'm here to tell you — **chase truth instead**.

Success fades. Money rots. Power corrupts. But truth? Truth liberates.

The truth is this: You are **nothing** — and that is your greatest power. When you strip away the labels, the expectations, and the lies — you return to **zero**, to the raw, unshaped, infinite version of yourself. From that zero, you can build **anything**. From that nothingness, you can become **everything**.

This book is a rebellion — a call to **unlearn** everything they made you believe.

It's for the misfits, the dreamers, and the restless minds that never felt at home in this world. It's for the souls who feel the weight of the system but know, deep down, they were born to break it.

You don't need permission to be free. You don't need validation to be powerful. You don't need the system to tell you who you are.

Burn the false self. Reject the illusion. Reclaim your mind.

This isn't just a book. It's a battle cry — a war against the lies that hold you prisoner.

The chains are tightening. The crowd is moving. **Will you follow, or will you rise?**

The revolution isn't coming. **It starts now — with you.**

— Saurabh Katiyar

Table of Contents

Chapter 1: The Illusion of Identity — Breaking Free from Mental Slavery 1

Chapter 2: The Awakening — Destroying the False Self .. 6

Chapter 3: Untouchable — Beyond Fear, Beyond the System 10

Chapter 4: The Creator — Building Your Own Reality ...14

Chapter 5: The Torchbearer — Leading the Lost 19

Chapter 6: Becoming the System's Nightmare 23

Chapter 7: Building the New World 28

Chapter 8: The True Vision of Life — Beyond the Illusion of Success 33

Chapter 9: The Rise of the Conscious Rebel 38

Chapter 10: Building a Life of Purpose 42

Chapter 11: Zero to Infinity — Becoming the Light 45

PART -1
The mirror within :
Self-awakening begins

Chapter 1:
The Illusion of Identity — Breaking Free from Mental Slavery

"The only real prison is fear, and the only real freedom is freedom from fear." — Aung San Suu Kyi

The Birth of Purity

When you were born, you were pure — an empty slate, free from the weight of labels, expectations, and fears. You were a limitless source of potential. You didn't know your name, your religion, your caste, or even what success or failure meant. You simply *were*. A being of infinite possibilities.

But soon after, the world began to write on that slate. Society, family, school, religion, and the system shaped you into what they wanted you to become. They gave you a name, a caste, and a nationality — and told you that these things define you. You were taught that your worth depends on your grades, your job, your wealth, and how well you fit into the roles designed by others.

Suddenly, the limitless being within you was replaced by a manufactured identity. You became a reflection of societal expectations — not your true self.

The Chains of Conditioning

"The greatest enemy of knowledge is not ignorance; it is the illusion of knowledge." — Stephen Hawking

From childhood, you were fed rules, beliefs, and ideas that were never yours to begin with. If you score less, you're a failure. If you don't secure a high-paying job, you're useless. If you think differently from the crowd, you're wrong.

This is not education; it's conditioning — a systematic way of turning a powerful, free human being into a submissive cog in a machine.

Fear and greed were planted deep within you:

- Fear of failure.
- Fear of being alone.
- Fear of disappointing others.
- Greed for success, status, and wealth.

These emotions became the driving force of your life. But who decided that these things define your worth? Did you? Or did the system?

The Manufactured Reality

Imagine this: A lion born and raised in a cage grows up believing the cage is its world. Even if the cage door is opened, the lion might never step out — because it doesn't know freedom exists. It believes the cage is where it belongs.

You are that lion.

Your cage is made of false beliefs, inherited identities, and societal pressures. And just like the lion, you may not even realize you're trapped.

But the truth is this entire reality — the one that says you must follow the crowd, obey the system, chase success, and fear failure — is man-made. It's an illusion.

Breaking Free: The Return to Zero

"He who controls others may be powerful, but he who has mastered himself is mightier still." — Lao Tzu

Real freedom begins when you *unlearn* what you were taught to believe about yourself. It starts when you break the mental chains that bind you.

To truly awaken, you must first return to **zero** — the state of purity you were born with, free from false identities. This doesn't mean you erase everything you know. It means you question everything you've accepted blindly.

- Are you really your name, caste, or nationality?
- Are you only as good as your grades or job title?
- Are you living your life — or someone else's dream?

When you shed these manufactured identities, you don't become *nothing* — you become **limitless** again. Zero isn't emptiness; it's a foundation of endless possibilities.

From Zero to Infinity

The moment you return to zero, a new journey begins — a journey towards **infinity**. It's the path of self-discovery and mastery.

Infinity doesn't mean having no limits in the material sense; it means understanding that you are not bound by fear, greed, or false identities. You become the creator of your own identity — one built on your **truth**, not the system's lies.

Look at the greatest minds and revolutionaries in history — Albert Einstein, Nikola Tesla, Leonardo da Vinci, Gautama Buddha, Socrates, and even modern trailblazers like Elon

Musk. They weren't shaped by the crowd. They stood apart, questioned the norms, and broke free from mental slavery.

They dared to return to zero — and from that, they created their own infinity.

The Choice is Yours

"The man who follows the crowd will usually go no further than the crowd. The man who walks alone is likely to find himself in places no one has ever been." — Albert Einstein

So now the decision lies before you:

- Will you remain a product of conditioning, a slave to the system — living for others' approval?
- Or will you strip away the false layers, return to zero, and build your true self from scratch?

The path won't be easy. You'll face resistance from those who fear your awakening. But once you break free, no one can control you again.

Is it time to choose: slavery or infinity?

Your journey begins now.

Chapter 2: The Awakening — Destroying the False Self

"It is no measure of health to be well-adjusted to a profoundly sick society." — Jiddu Krishna Murti

The First Fracture

The moment you decide to break free from the illusion, a crack forms in the false identity you've worn for so long. It's unsettling. The comfort of the familiar — even if it's a prison — begins to call you back. The crowd looks safe. The system feels secure. But deep down, you now know the truth: **it was never real.**

You've seen the cage for what it is. Now, you stand at the edge, staring into the unknown. The path ahead is not paved by society; it's raw, untamed, and yours to create.

This is where the real war begins — not with the world, but within yourself.

The False Self: Your Greatest Enemy

"The worst loneliness is to not be comfortable with yourself." — Mark Twain

The false self is the version of you that the world created. It's made of labels, expectations, and fear. It's the voice that tells you:

- "You must fit in to be accepted."
- "You need more money to be respected."

- "You must achieve success to be worthy."
- "If you fail, you're nothing."

This voice isn't yours — it belongs to the system. But it speaks from inside you, pretending to be your thoughts. It's clever, manipulative, and relentless.

The false self is afraid of one thing: **truth.** Because truth burns it to the ground.

The Collapse of Lies

Imagine a tower built on a foundation of lies. Every brick represents a belief you never questioned:

- "Good grades define intelligence."
- "A high-paying job equals success."
- "Marriage, children, and a house equal a complete life."
- "Sacrifice your dreams for stability."
- "Follow the rules, and you'll be happy."

What happens when you realize the foundation is rotten? The tower collapses. And for a while, you feel lost, broken, and empty. But this collapse isn't the end — it's the beginning.

Because only when the false self-dies can the **real you** emerge.

The Fire of Transformation

"You have to die a few times before you can really live." — *Charles Bukowski*

The destruction of the false self feels like death because, in a way, it is. It's the death of who you were told to be — and the birth of who you truly are.

This transformation is not comfortable. You'll face:

- **Loneliness** — because you'll no longer fit in with the crowd.
- **Fear** — because the future is now unwritten.
- **Doubt** — because the old voices will try to pull you back.

But something extraordinary happens when you push through this fire: you realize that the pain wasn't coming from breaking free — it was from holding on to a false life that never belonged to you.

The Rise of the True Self

Once the false self crumbles, the real you — the one buried beneath years of conditioning — begins to rise. This version of you doesn't seek approval. It doesn't chase empty success or fear failure. It simply exists in its purest form: free, fearless, and limitless.

This is the moment you return to zero — not as a blank slate, but as a conscious creator.

Zero is now your weapon. It's the place where you shed the past, reject the lies, and build yourself from truth. And from zero, infinity starts to unfold.

Reclaiming Your Power

"The most courageous act is still to think for yourself. Aloud." — Coco Chanel

You've been conditioned to believe power belongs to those above you — governments, corporations, religions, systems. But what if the greatest power was always within you?

The system survives because people obey. It collapses when people **think.**

When you reclaim your mind, you become uncontrollable. No longer can fear, guilt, or social pressure manipulate you. You see the world for what it truly is: a stage where most people are acting out roles they never chose.

But you're no longer an actor. You're the writer of your own script.

The World Fears the Awakened

Be prepared — the world won't celebrate your awakening. People trapped in the system will see your freedom as a threat. They'll call you reckless, arrogant, or even crazy.

Why? Because your very existence becomes proof that the cage isn't real.

When one person breaks free, they expose the illusion. And the crowd hates nothing more than being reminded of their chains.

But remember this: **Their fear is not your burden.**

Chapter 3:
Untouchable — Beyond Fear, Beyond the System

"The secret to happiness is freedom... and the secret to freedom is courage." — Thucydides

The Illusion of Fear

Fear is the most powerful weapon ever created. Not guns, not bombs — fear. It's invisible, yet it controls billions of lives. It keeps people in jobs they hate, in relationships that suffocate them, and in systems that exploit them.

But what is fear, really?

It's a prediction — a hallucination of pain that hasn't happened yet. The system feeds you this hallucination from birth:

- *"If you don't obey, you'll suffer."*
- *"If you step out of line, you'll be punished."*
- *"If you chase your own path, you'll fail."*

And so, you obey. Not because you want to, but because you're terrified of the alternative.

But here's the truth: **The fear isn't real.** It never was. It's a story designed to keep you weak and compliant.

The Death of Fear

What happens when you face fear head-on — when you refuse to run?

It dies.

Fear thrives on avoidance. It grows when you hide from it. But the moment you stare it down, it crumbles. Like a shadow exposed to light, it has no substance of its own.

The system doesn't want you to know this. It relies on your fear to survive. Because a person without fear is a person who cannot be controlled.

When you kill fear, you become untouchable.

The System's Last Trick: Guilt

Fear is only half the trap. The other half is guilt.

If fear fails to stop you, the system whispers another lie:

"You're selfish for breaking free." "You owe something to your family, your society, your culture." "Who are you to think you deserve more?"

This is emotional manipulation disguised as morality. Guilt keeps you in chains by making you feel like a traitor for wanting freedom.

But let's break this illusion too: You owe the system nothing. Not your time, not your energy, not your life.

Your existence is not a debt.

The Liberation of Selfishness

The word *"selfish"* has been twisted into an insult — but it's a weapon you can reclaim. Real selfishness isn't about harming others. It's about having the courage to prioritize your truth over the system's expectations.

Selfishness means saying:

- **"My life belongs to me — not society."**

- **"My dreams matter more than their approval."**
- **"I choose my path, even if I walk it alone."**

The system calls this arrogance. But the awakened know it as **self-respect**.

Becoming Untouchable

To become untouchable, you must undergo one final transformation:

You must detach from everything the system uses to control you — fear, guilt, approval, and even identity.

1. Detach from Fear: Realize that fear is a liar. The worst-case scenario is never as bad as a life wasted in chains.

2. Detach from Guilt: Guilt is a weapon to keep you small. Your life is yours. Full stop.

3. Detach from Approval: Approval is a drug. The more you crave it, the more powerless you become. Let go of the need to be liked.

4. Detach from Identity: The labels you were given — student, employee, citizen, success, failure — are cages. Who are you beyond those labels?

When you let go of these attachments, the system loses its grip. You become an anomaly — someone who can't be manipulated, frightened, or shamed.

The system fears this version of you. Because an untouchable person is no longer a pawn — they're a force.

The World Beyond the System

What's left when fear, guilt, and false identity are gone?

Freedom.

Not the shallow, advertised freedom of the system — the kind that comes with a price tag. **Real freedom.** The kind that no one can give or take away from you.

It's the freedom to think without limits. To create without permission. To live without apology.

This freedom is terrifying to those still trapped. They'll look at you and see rebellion, danger, even madness. But you'll know the truth:

You didn't rebel. You returned to yourself.

You didn't break the system. You walked away from it.

You didn't go mad. You woke up.

The Awakening is Contagious

The most dangerous thing about an untouchable person isn't their freedom — it's that their freedom is contagious.

When people see you living without fear, without guilt, without needing approval, they'll start to question their own chains. Your existence will become a crack in their reality. A crack that, one day, might shatter it completely.

And that's the system's greatest nightmare.

Chapter 4:
The Creator —
Building Your Own Reality

"The best way to predict the future is to create it." — Peter Drucker

The Illusion of a Ready-Made World

The system sells you a prepackaged life. A neat, predictable path laid out like a conveyor belt:

- Get good grades.
- Get a degree.
- Get a job.
- Get married.
- Buy a house.
- Retire.
- Die.

This path isn't for your happiness — it's for the system's stability. It needs obedient workers, predictable consumers, and docile citizens. A life designed by someone else isn't a life — it's a program.

But now you've broken free. The program is exposed. And the question hits you: **What now?**

The answer is both terrifying and exhilarating: **Now, you create.**

The Power of Creation

"You are not a drop in the ocean. You are the entire ocean in a drop." — Rumi

The system convinced you that you're powerless. That life happens *to* you, and your only job is to react.

That was a lie.

You are a creator. Not in the poetic, motivational sense— in the literal sense. Every belief, every action, every choice reshapes your reality. When you strip away the false self, you're left with raw creative power.

But creation isn't easy. It requires unlearning everything you were taught about what's possible.

Step 1: Destroy the Old Blueprint

Before you build, you must **demolish.**

The old blueprint — the system's version of "success" — is still lurking in your subconscious. Burn it. Every trace. Ask yourself:

- Would I still want this if nobody could see me achieve it?
- Does this goal excite my soul, or just impress others?
- Am I chasing this because I want it, or because I'm afraid of what happens if I don't?

If your goal is rooted in fear, guilt, or the desire for approval, it's not yours. Let it go.

Step 2: Redefine Success

Society defines success by status — job titles, income, possessions, and popularity. This is a distraction.

Real success is simpler: **freedom, purpose, and joy.**

- **Freedom:** The ability to choose how you spend your time — not trading your life for a paycheck.
- **Purpose:** Waking up with a reason beyond survival. A mission that makes your existence matter.
- **Joy:** Not the fleeting high of consumerism, but the deep satisfaction of living on your terms.

Define success for yourself — or the world will define it for you.

Step 3: Build Without Permission

The system teaches you to wait for permission:

- Permission to start a business.
- Permission to speak your truth.
- Permission to live differently.

Permission is a myth. No one is coming to validate you. The moment you stop waiting and start doing so, you reclaim your power.

Want to start a project? Start it. Want to pursue a passion? Pursue it. Want to reinvent yourself? Reinvent.

Stop asking, **"Am I allowed to do this?"** And start asking, **"Who's going to stop me?"**

Step 4: Create from Zero

You've returned to zero — the place beyond fear, guilt, and false identity. Now, create from that place.

- **If money didn't matter, what would you build?**

- **If you weren't afraid of judgment, what would you create?**
- **If you had nothing to lose, who would you become?**

Create like a child — without overthinking, without seeking approval, without limits. Children don't build sandcastles for praise. They build because creation is its own reward.

Step 5: Embrace the Chaos

Creation is messy. The system teaches you to fear mistakes — but mistakes are proof you're doing something real. Failure isn't the opposite of success; it's part of the process.

The difference between creators and spectators? **Creators keep going.**

When the Wright brothers failed, they didn't stop — they adjusted the design. When Edison's lightbulb failed a thousand times, he didn't quit — he learned.

The system tells you failure is the end. Creators know failure is feedback.

The Creator's Mindset: No One is Coming to Save You

Here's the raw truth: **No one is coming to save you.**

Not the government. Not your boss. Not your parents. Not society.

If you want freedom, you must build it yourself. No one hands over power — you take it.

This isn't cruel. It's liberating. Because when you stop waiting for a saviour, you realize you never needed one.

Your Reality, Your Rules

The system wants you to believe reality is fixed. That life is a script you must follow.

But reality is malleable. People who reshaped the world — inventors, artists, entrepreneurs, revolutionaries— weren't special. They were awake. They realized the script was optional.

The only difference between you and them is the decision to create.

So, what will you create?

A business that breaks the Mold? A career built on passion, not pay checks? A life so authentic it becomes a rebellion in itself?

The system fears the creator more than anything — because creators don't follow rules. They write their own.

Chapter 5:
The Torchbearer — Leading the Lost

"Be the light that helps others see." — *Unknown*

The Prison of the Mind

Imagine a group of prisoners chained inside a dark cave, facing a wall. All they see are shadows projected by a fire behind them. To them, the shadows are reality — they know nothing else. This is Plato's Allegory of the Cave.

One day, a prisoner breaks free. He stumbles into the light outside the cave, blinded at first, but eventually he sees the world as it truly is — vibrant, limitless, and beautiful. When he returns to the cave to free the others, they mock him. They're too afraid to believe him. The shadows are all they know.

This is the world we live in.

Most people are trapped in their own mental caves — conditioned to believe the shadows are reality. Their "truth" is what the system feeds them: a job title, a pay check, a social status, a life measured by approval.

You were once one of them.

But now, you've broken free. You've seen the light. The question is: will you walk away — or will you return to help those still chained in darkness?

The Fear of Freedom

Freedom sounds beautiful — but it terrifies those who've never tasted it.

Picture a lion born in a cage. It's fed every day, safe from danger. One day, the cage door is left open. Does the lion run? No. It stays inside. The wild is unknown and unpredictable. The cage may be a prison — but it's familiar.

Humans are the same. People cling to the system not because they love it but because they fear what lies beyond it.

That's why leading the lost isn't about pushing them. It's about **awakening** them.

Step 1: Plant the Seed of Doubt

The first step isn't to tell people they're slaves. They won't believe you. Their identity is built on the system's lies — attacking that will only make them defensive.

Instead, plant questions that make them think:

- *"Why do you think success is tied to a job title?"*
- *"Who taught you that failure is something to fear?"*
- *"What would you do if money weren't an issue?"*

The mind rejects force but welcomes curiosity. Plant the seed, and let it grow.

Step 2: Show, Don't Tell

People don't follow words — they follow examples.

Be the living proof that freedom is possible. Show them what it looks like to live without fear, without guilt, without needing permission.

- **If you quit the job you hated and built your own path— they'll notice.**
- **If you stop seeking approval and start speaking your truth— they'll notice.**

- **If you live boldly, unapologetically— they'll notice.**

The system teaches people to obey. Seeing someone who doesn't obey but thrives? That's dangerous. That's inspiring.

Step 3: Break the False Promises

The system keeps people loyal with promises:

- *"Work hard, and you'll be successful."*
- *"Follow the rules, and you'll be safe."*
- *"Stay in line, and you'll be happy."*

Expose the truth: these promises are bait — and the hook is control.

- People who work hard for others often end up broke.
- People who follow the rules are replaceable.
- People who chase status end up empty.

The system doesn't reward loyalty — it exploits it. Once people see this, the chains loosen.

Step 4: Ignite Their Inner Fire

Freedom is not given. It's claimed.

Help people remember their own power — the fire buried beneath fear and conditioning.

- *"What did you love before the world told you who to be?"*
- *"What's one thing you've always wanted to do — but never had the courage to try?"*
- *"Who could you become if nothing held you back?"*

The goal isn't to make them follow you. The goal is to make them follow **themselves.**

Step 5: Prepare for Resistance

Not everyone wants to be free.

Some will fight to protect their chains — they'll call you reckless, selfish, even dangerous. Why? Because your freedom threatens their illusions.

But a few — a rare, brave few — will hear you. They'll see the truth. And once they do, they'll never unsee it.

These are the ones you're fighting for.

The Chain Reaction

Every awakened mind is a spark. And sparks start wildfires.

When you break free, you inspire others to do the same. And when they break free, they'll inspire others. The system survives on obedience — but all it takes is enough people who refuse to obey.

You don't need to save everyone. You just need to save **one.**

The rest will follow.

Chapter 6: Becoming the System's Nightmare

"The most dangerous man is the one who has nothing to lose." — Tupac Shakur

The System's Greatest Fear

The system doesn't fear protests, revolutions, or rebellion. It expects those — and knows how to crush them.

What it truly fears is the awakened individual — someone who no longer needs the system at all.

Why? Because a person who doesn't need the system can't be controlled.

- You can't be bribed with money when you define your own success.
- You can't be blackmailed with fear when you're no longer afraid of failure or judgment.
- You can't be manipulated with approval when you no longer seek permission to exist.

You become unpredictable. Unstoppable. A walking glitch in their program.

It's time to stop playing defence and start playing offense.

The Weapon of the Unstoppable Mind

The system's control is rooted in one thing: **fear.**

- Fear of poverty keeps you at a job you hate.
- Fear of judgment keeps you quiet.

- Fear of failure keeps you from trying.

The system is powerless against someone who no longer fears these things.

So, how do you become that person? You must dismantle fear from the inside out.

Step 1: Embrace the Worst-Case Scenario

Fear thrives on uncertainty. The unknown terrifies the mind. But what happens when you stop running from the worst-case scenario — and face it head-on?

Ask yourself:

- *"What if I fail and lose everything?"* — You'll start over, wiser and stronger.
- *"What if they judge me?"* — Their opinions don't pay your bills.
- *"What if I'm wrong?"* — You'll learn, adapt, and try again.

Fear dies the moment you stop avoiding it. Once you embrace the worst-case scenario, you realize it's survivable — and that makes you untouchable.

Step 2: Stop Playing by Their Rules

The system's rules were never designed for your success — they were designed for its survival.

Break them.

- They say you need a degree? Build skills instead.
- They say you need a 9-to-5 job? Create your own income.

- They say you need to follow the safe path? Define your own path.

The moment you stop playing by their rules, you become a rogue variable — a wild card they can't predict or control.

Step 3: Own Your Identity

The system gave you a label — student, employee, citizen — to keep you small and manageable.

Rip it off.

You are not your job. You are not your past. You are not your mistakes. You are a creator, a force of nature, a mind capable of reshaping reality.

The system's nightmare isn't a crowd of rebels — it's an individual who has awakened to their true identity.

Step 4: Become Self-Sufficient

The system keeps you dependent — on employers, institutions, and validation.

Take that power back.

- Learn to make money without a boss.
- Build skills that make you valuable in any environment.
- Master your mind so you no longer crave external approval.

The less you need from the system, the less it can control you.

Step 5: Turn Pain into Power

The system wants you to believe that pain, failure, and rejection are signs you should quit.

That's another lie.

Pain is fuel. Every setback, every loss, every betrayal — it's all raw energy waiting to be converted into power.

- They laughed at you? Let that sharpen your focus.
- Did they doubt you? Let that harden your resolve.
- They tried to break you? Let that forge your strength.

The system fears people who turn pain into power — because those people are impossible to break.

Step 6: Become the Hunter, Not the Hunted

Most people spend their lives running — from fear, from failure, from the system's judgment.

Stop running. Turn around.

- Chase what scares you.
- Attack what holds you back.
- Confront the lies head-on.

When the system realizes you're no longer prey — that you've become the hunter — it panics. Because hunters create their own rules.

The System Can't Stop an Idea Whose Time Has Come

The truth is, the system is already cracking. It's slow, outdated, and terrifying of the individuals waking up.

Every awakened mind is a virus to the system — a glitch that spreads. One turns into ten. Ten turns into thousands. And soon, the system is overwhelmed.

You are not just one person. You are a spark in a forest ready to burn.

The system can silence a person — but it can't stop an idea whose time has come.

Chapter 7: Building the New World

"The best way to predict the future is to create it." — *Peter Drucker*

From Ashes to Blueprints

The old world was built on lies — and you've watched it burn.

But what now? Freedom isn't enough. Being free without a vision is like escaping a prison only to wander in the desert. We can't stop at destruction — we must **create.**

It's time to build a new world — one that serves humanity, not the system.

But how do you build a world from nothing?

You start the way all great creators do — by imagining the impossible.

Step 1: Dare to Imagine the Impossible

Every great civilization, every technological marvel, every revolutionary idea was once mocked as impossible.

- The Wright brothers were told humans would never fly. Now, planes carry millions every day.
- Nikola Tesla dreamed of wireless electricity in a world that barely understood wired power. Today, Wi-Fi connects the world.
- Martin Luther King Jr. envisioned a world where people were judged by their character, not their

colour— and shook the foundations of an entire nation.

The system teaches you to think *practically,* to *be realistic,* and to *know your limits.*

Ignore that.

The new world begins with those brave enough to imagine what doesn't exist yet.

Close your eyes and ask yourself, *"What would the world look like if fear, greed, and control no longer ruled it?"*

Let your mind run wild. Imagine a world where

- People chase purpose, not pay checks.
- Education awakens minds instead of moulding them.
- Technology serves humanity, not corporations.
- Compassion fuels leadership, not power.

The system calls this utopian nonsense. But the system's greatest fear is that you might actually build it.

Step 2: Become the Architect of Your Own Reality

The truth they never taught you? You are not a prisoner of the world — you are the architect.

Most people live in a reality designed for them by others. Their beliefs, habits, and even desires are programmed by the system.

But architects don't live in someone else's blueprint — they create their own.

Ask yourself:

- *"What kind of life do I want to live — not the life I was told to want?"*
- *"What kind of work excites me — not what pays the most?"*
- *"What values do I live by — not what society says is right?"*

The new world starts when individuals design their own reality — and stop living someone else's.

Step 3: Rebuild the Foundations of Power

The old world is built on power concentrated in the hands of a few — governments, corporations, and institutions.

The new world distributes power to the many — to the people.

- **Decentralized knowledge:** No more gatekeepers deciding who gets access to education and information. Knowledge must flow freely.
- **Decentralized wealth:** Break the chains of the traditional job market. Create systems where individuals generate value on their own terms.
- **Decentralized leadership:** Leaders shouldn't rise through manipulation or money — they should emerge from wisdom, compassion, and vision.

Power doesn't belong to the few. It belongs to the creators, the thinkers, the rebels — it belongs to you.

Step 4: Build Without Permission

The system wants you to believe you need permission — from society, from authorities, from institutions — to create something new.

You don't.

- **You don't need permission to start a movement.**
- **You don't need permission to build a business that challenges the old ways.**
- **You don't need permission to invent, create, lead, or inspire.**

The greatest builders in history never asked for permission. They saw what the world lacked — and they built it themselves.

The system's power vanishes the moment you realize you were free all along.

Step 5: Inspire Others to Build

A single spark doesn't create a wildfire — but a thousand sparks do.

The new world isn't built by one person. It's built when millions wake up and realize they can build too.

Be the spark for someone else.

- Share your ideas openly — don't hoard them.
- Lift others as you rise — a true leader creates more leaders.
- Show, don't tell — let your life be proof that the old world isn't the only way.

The most powerful revolutions start when ordinary people realize they can create extraordinary change.

The New World Awaits

The old world is dying. Let it.

The new world is waiting — but it won't build itself.

It's time to stop waiting for permission. It's time to stop hoping for change. It's time to create the world they told you was impossible.

The question now is no longer *"What if?"*

The question is, *"What's next?"*

Chapter 8: The True Vision of Life — Beyond the Illusion of Success

"Be the change that you wish to see in the world." — Mahatma Gandhi

The Mirage of Success

From the moment you could understand language, the world sold you an illusion — that success is money, status, and power. They made you believe that a bigger house, a faster car, and a fancier title equal a better life.

But have you ever stopped to ask— *Why do the richest people often feel the emptiest? Why do powerful leaders crave more power even after having everything? Why do celebrities with millions of fans still fall into depression?*

It's because they chased the illusion of success, not the truth of fulfillment.

True success is not what you have — it's **who you become.**

Mahatma Gandhi once laid out **seven social sins** — a guide to what destroys society and individual souls. Let's break them down and discover how they apply to your life, and how living beyond these sins shapes you into a true leader.

---

1. Wealth Without Work

The system glorifies easy money — quick schemes, shortcuts, overnight success. Social media flaunts luxury cars, designer clothes, and private jets, often without showing the work behind them.

But wealth without effort is hollow. It breeds entitlement and corruption.

Example: Lottery winners often end up bankrupt or miserable within a few years. They gained wealth but lacked the mindset to sustain it. Contrast this with Elon Musk or Steve Jobs — who built empires from nothing, working day and night on their visions.

The Lesson: Wealth isn't evil — but how you earn it defines whether it strengthens or corrupts you. True wealth is built on value, innovation, and service.

2. Pleasure Without Conscience

Modern society worships pleasure — instant gratification, endless entertainment, indulgence without limits.

But pleasure without moral grounding leads to addiction, emptiness, and destruction.

Example: Look at Rome's fall — an empire that once ruled the world crumbled because it gave in to indulgence and excess. The pursuit of pleasure blinded leaders to the rot within their society.

The Lesson: Enjoy life's pleasures — but never at the expense of your values, your people, or your integrity.

3. Knowledge Without Character

We live in an age of unlimited information. You can learn anything in seconds.

But knowledge without moral character is dangerous. It creates manipulators, tyrants, and people who weaponize intelligence to control others.

Example: Hitler was brilliant — a master strategist and communicator. But his lack of empathy and humanity turned that knowledge into a tool for genocide.

The Lesson: Intelligence must be tempered by empathy and wisdom. A brilliant mind with a wicked heart is a ticking time bomb.

4. Commerce Without Morality

The system rewards profits — no matter the cost. Companies exploit workers, destroy nature, and deceive customers in the name of "business."

Example: Fast fashion brands rake in billions while underpaying laborers in sweatshops. Meanwhile, companies like **Patagonia** thrive by prioritizing ethics — paying fair wages, using sustainable materials, and protecting the environment.

The Lesson: Business isn't about squeezing maximum profit — it's about creating value while staying true to moral principles.

5. Science Without Humanity

Technology evolves faster than ever — but at what cost? AI, genetic engineering, nuclear power — all powerful tools, but deadly without ethical control.

Example: The creation of the atomic bomb was a scientific triumph — yet it led to unimaginable destruction in Hiroshima and Nagasaki.

The Lesson: Science must serve humanity, not overpower it. Progress without compassion is regression.

6. Worship Without Sacrifice

People pray, chant, and follow rituals — but forget the core of spirituality: selflessness and service.

Example: Gandhi fasted for peace. Mother Teresa left comfort to serve the poor. Meanwhile, many today worship for appearances, not inner transformation.

The Lesson: True spirituality isn't about rituals — it's about sacrificing ego, greed, and hatred to serve humanity.

7. Politics Without Principle

Power attracts the wrong people — those who crave control, not those who seek to serve.

Example: Nelson Mandela endured 27 years in prison but emerged with forgiveness, not vengeance — leading South Africa to democracy. He stood by his principles, even when it cost him everything.

The Lesson: True leadership isn't about popularity — it's about standing for what's right, even when it's hard.

The Blueprint for a Perfect Life

A perfect life isn't perfect. It's filled with challenges, pain, and failures. But it's a life driven by purpose, not illusion.

- **Define your values** — and never compromise them.
- **Create more than you consume.**
- **Serve others — because fulfillment grows when shared.**

- **Lead with integrity, even when no one's watching.**
- **Pursue growth, not comfort.**

A great leader isn't the loudest or the richest. A great leader is the one who lights the path for others — even when walking through darkness themselves.

"Your beliefs become your thoughts, Your thoughts become your words, Your words become your actions, Your actions become your habits, Your habits become your values, Your values become your destiny." — Mahatma Gandhi

Chapter 9:
The Rise of the Conscious Rebel

"The mind that opens to a new idea never returns to its original size." — Albert Einstein

The world doesn't need more followers. It needs thinkers, builders, and rebels — people who refuse to live under the weight of old, broken systems. By now, you've stripped away the false identities forced upon you. But shedding the past isn't enough. You must rise from the ashes of conditioning — not just as a free person, but as a conscious rebel.

What is a Conscious Rebel?

A rebel without purpose is just noise. But a conscious rebel is different — they think deeply, act wisely, and break the right rules. They don't rebel for rebellion's sake; they rebel against ignorance, injustice, and falsehood.

Ask yourself:

- Why do you believe what you believe?
- Are your goals truly yours, or were they planted by society?
- If success wasn't measured by money or status, what would you pursue?

The conscious rebel challenges these questions — and seeks answers.

The System Thrives on Your Fear

The system doesn't actually need your obedience. It needs your fear. Fear keeps you from asking the right questions. It keeps you glued to paths you never chose.

Example: Consider Galileo Galilei — condemned for proving the Earth revolves around the sun. The world wasn't afraid of his science; they were afraid of losing the lies they clung to. Galileo wasn't a rebel because he defied the church — he was a rebel because he refused to let fear silence the truth.

The Lesson: Fear isn't a sign to stop — it's a signal you're on the edge of something revolutionary.

Break the Chains of Approval

The greatest illusion society ever created is that you need its approval to be worthy.

Example: Vincent Van Gogh sold only one painting in his lifetime. He died poor, mocked, and misunderstood. Today, his art is priceless. Van Gogh wasn't a failure — the world simply wasn't ready for him. Imagine if he had stopped painting because society called him "mad."

The Lesson: The crowd is often wrong. Don't let its noise define your value.

The Philosophy of Rebellion

History's greatest thinkers weren't obedient. They weren't afraid to challenge dogma.

- **Socrates** questioned Athens' beliefs and was sentenced to death — but his ideas shaped Western philosophy.
- **Rosa Parks** refused to give up her bus seat — and sparked the Civil Rights Movement.
- **Nikola Tesla** rejected mainstream science and was ridiculed — yet his inventions power the modern world.

What would have happened if they chose comfort over conviction? The world doesn't need more spectators. It needs more Tesla, more Parks, more Socrates — and perhaps, more *you.*

Rebuild Your Mindset: The Rebel's Creed

1. **Question Everything:** Don't accept beliefs because they're popular. Test them. Break them. Keep only what stands.

2. **Embrace Discomfort:** Growth is painful. Comfort zones are death traps disguised as safe spaces.

3. **Think Long-Term:** The crowd chases instant rewards. Rebels build legacies that outlast them.

4. **Don't Fear Solitude:** Every rebel walks alone at some point. Solitude isn't loneliness — it's the forge where you find your true self.

5. **Lead by Example:** A conscious rebel doesn't tell people to wake up. They wake up first — and their light becomes a beacon for others.

The Final Call: Will You Rise?

At this point, the choice is yours.

You can return to the crowd — safe, silent, forgettable. Or you can rise — uncertain, challenged, but truly alive.

The world doesn't change when millions obey. It changes when one person stands up and says, *"This is wrong."*

Will you be that person?

"The ones who are crazy enough to think they can change the world are the ones who do." — Rob Siltanen

The path from zero to infinity has begun — and the world awaits your rebellion.

Chapter 10: Building a Life of Purpose

"He who has a way to live can bear almost any how." — Friedrich Nietzsche

A life without purpose is like a ship without a captain — drifting aimlessly. Success, money, fame — these are side effects, not destinations. The real journey starts when you stop asking, *"What can I get from life?"* and start asking, *"What can I give to life?"*

Why Most People Never Find Their Purpose

The truth is unsettling: most people never find their purpose because they never stop to look. They're too busy chasing shadows — jobs, social validation, fleeting pleasures — mistaking movement for progress.

Example: Picture a man climbing a ladder, only to realize it's leaning against the wrong wall. He reached the top, but what did he actually achieve? More money? More status? Emptiness disguised as success?

The Lesson: Purpose isn't about chasing — it's about creating. It's about building something that outlives you.

How to Discover Your Purpose

Finding your purpose isn't a one-time event. It's a relentless process of questioning, failing, and evolving. Here's a map:

1. **Identify Your Core Values:** What principles are non-negotiable to you? Honesty? Freedom?

Compassion? Your values are the compass that directs your purpose.

2. **Find What Angers You:** Purpose isn't always born from passion — sometimes it's born from outrage. What injustice makes your blood boil? What broken part of the world do you feel compelled to fix?

3. **Ask: What Would I Do If I Knew I Couldn't Fail?** Strip away the fear of failure and imagine your boldest self. That version of you holds the blueprint to your purpose.

4. **Look at Your Natural Talents:** What are you effortlessly good at? Often, your gifts align with your purpose.

5. **Serve Something Bigger Than Yourself:** True purpose isn't selfish. It uplifts others — a family, a community, even humanity itself.

The Philosophies of Purpose

Different thinkers, different eras — yet they converge on a singular truth: life's meaning isn't given; it's created.

- **Stoicism** — Purpose is found in virtue: living with courage, wisdom, justice, and self-control.
- **Existentialism** — Life has no pre-assigned meaning; we must forge our own.
- **Buddhism** — Purpose is found by ending suffering — both our own and others'.

- **Ikigai** (Japanese philosophy) — Purpose lies at the intersection of what you love, what you're good at, what the world needs, and what you can be paid for.

Example: Viktor Frankl, a Holocaust survivor, endured unimaginable suffering. His conclusion? Those who survived weren't the strongest or healthiest — they were the ones with a clear sense of purpose, a reason to keep living.

Choose your philosophy, but let purpose guide your every action.

Purpose Over Pleasure: The Hidden Reward

The world glorifies pleasure — quick hits of dopamine from likes, views, and temporary highs. Purpose is harder. It demands sacrifice. But it gives something pleasure never can: fulfilment.

Example: Elon Musk didn't create SpaceX to make billions — he wanted to make humanity a multi-planetary species. The Wright brothers didn't invent flight for fame — they dreamed of breaking humanity's limits.

The Lesson: Pleasure fades. Purpose fuels you for a lifetime.

Chapter 11:
Zero to Infinity — Becoming the Light

"The one who conquers himself is greater than he who conquers a thousand men in battle." — Buddha

This is the final transformation — from seeker to leader, from follower to light. It's time to stop searching and start becoming.

The World Doesn't Need More Leaders — It Needs More Lights

A true leader isn't someone who commands. It's someone who illuminates — someone who inspires others to awaken.

Example: Mahatma Gandhi didn't lead with force — he led with moral clarity. He didn't say, *"Follow me."* He said, *"Be the change."* The people followed his light.

The Lesson: Leadership isn't about power — it's about responsibility.

The Five Pillars of Becoming the Light

1. **Self-Mastery:** Before you can change the world, you must master yourself. Your thoughts, habits, and emotions must obey you — not control you.

2. **Radical Integrity:** In a world drowning in lies, truth is revolutionary. Speak it. Live it. Even when it's uncomfortable.

3. **Relentless Compassion:** Strength without compassion creates tyrants. Compassion without strength creates victims. The balance makes you unstoppable.
4. **Fearless Action:** Knowing what's right isn't enough. Do it — even when you're scared, especially when you're scared.
5. **Legacy Thinking:** Every action plants a seed. Will your seeds grow forests... or weeds?

The Final Truth: You Are the Revolution

The system won't fix itself. The crowd won't wake up on its own. But you — you now hold the knowledge, the understanding, and the fire to spark change.

This book wasn't meant to inspire you. It was meant to **awaken** you.

Example: Imagine standing on your deathbed. Will you look back with regret — or pride? The answer depends on what you do next.

The Lesson: Don't wait for permission to live fully. The world needs you now — not someday.

"The privilege of a lifetime is to become who you truly are."
— Carl Jung

Now go. Create. Lead. Become infinity.

PART -2

The mirror expands-
Seeing the world with awakened eyes

Content

The Dirty Game of Politics 49

Humanity Above All 53

Making Life Meaningful..58

The True Purpose of Life: A Journey Within 64

The Education System: From Factories of Obedience
to Foundries of Humanity..68

Build a legacy, not just a resume.......................................75

The Best Way to Predict the Future of a Nation is by
Looking at Its Youth..81

The Choice: The Unseen Power Shaping Your Life 87

Togetherness: The Power of Unity....................................91

Clarity: The Foundation of Peak Performance..................94

Civic Sense: The Backbone of a Thriving Society..........101

The Dirty Game of Politics

They divide us — and we let them.

We argue over religion, caste, and politics like puppets while they pull the strings from behind their velvet curtains. Where did our logic go? Where did our courage hide? The truth is bitter —we've been conditioned to live like slaves, fooled into believing that obedience is patriotism and silence is wisdom.

Our leaders — old men with old minds — sit comfortably on thrones built from our hard-earned money. They promised us education, jobs, healthcare, justice, and safety — but delivered only speeches and scandals. Their lives will end soon, but the chaos they leave behind will be ours to inherit.

Meanwhile, what are we doing? Scrolling endlessly, lost in reels and distractions, watching life pass us by. We — the youth — were meant to be the fire that forges a new nation. Instead, we're flickering embers, hypnotized by screens, blind to the power we hold.

It's time to stop waiting for someone else to fix this broken system. No messiah is coming. No leader will save us. **We are the leaders we've been waiting for.**

Why the Youth Must Take Over

Politics — once meant to serve the people — has mutated into a theatre of deception. Those in power no longer lead; they manipulate. The politicians we see today are not visionaries but performers — selling dreams and delivering despair. They divide us into castes, religions, and economic classes, not for unity, but for control. They dangle bait in the form of free electricity, rations, and petty pensions — breadcrumbs to keep us satisfied, distracted, and obedient.

But what do we get in return? Broken promises, crumbling infrastructure, skyrocketing unemployment, and a future mortgaged to corruption. Why? Because the ones making the decisions are relics of a bygone era — disconnected from the realities we face today.

The Age of Misrepresentation

In a world driven by innovation and youthful energy, how can leaders in their 70s, 80s, or even 90s possibly represent the dreams and struggles of a generation they don't understand? Why is it that we have a minimum age to contest elections but no maximum age to step down? A 20-year-old can't lead, but an 80-year-old can?

"Age is no guarantee of wisdom, and youth is no guarantee of ignorance." — a truth we must embrace. The youth, with fresh perspectives and boundless energy, should be at the forefront of change — not sidelined as mere voters.

We're told we're too young, too inexperienced to lead — yet we're old enough to fight wars, pay taxes, and inherit the debt created by these so-called leaders. If we're trusted to die for our country, why are we not trusted to govern it?

Philosophy of Politics — What It Should Be, and What It's Become

Politics, as envisioned by great thinkers like Aristotle and Plato, was meant to be an instrument of justice, a mechanism to ensure the well-being of the people. Plato spoke of philosopher-kings — rulers who govern not for personal gain, but for the collective good. Today, we have the opposite: career politicians who treat power as a family heirloom.

Mahatma Gandhi once said, *"The best way to find yourself is to lose yourself in the service of others."* But modern politicians seem to have rewritten this to: *"The best way to secure power is to serve your own interests."*

We, the youth, must reclaim politics — not as a dirty word, but as a noble pursuit. We must rise, not to rule, but to lead with integrity.

Why Are We Still a "Developing" Country?

Decade after decade, the same speeches echo —"India is a developing nation." Why? With a population of over 1.4 billion, rich in resources, talent, and ambition, what's holding us back?

The answer is simple: corruption and outdated leadership.

How can we progress when our leaders prioritize votes over vision? When development plans are buried beneath red tape and greed? When public money fuels personal empires rather than national growth? A country isn't poor when it lacks resources — it's poor when those resources are stolen by those who were meant to protect them.

The Role of Youth in Politics — A Revolution Waiting to Ignite

We are not just the future. We are the present. Climate change, unemployment, education reform, healthcare — these aren't issues for tomorrow. They're crises now, and they demand voices that refuse to be silenced.

Young people across the world have proven their power. Greta Thunberg shook world leaders on climate change.

Malala Yousafzai defied oppression to fight for education. Why are we waiting for heroes when we could become them?

We have the technology, the global connections, and the passion to reshape politics. But first, we must shed the apathy that's been programmed into us. **We must stop voting for freebies and start voting for change.** Free rations, pensions, and handouts are not solutions —they're traps. They keep us dependent and powerless.

A vote is not a transaction; it's a responsibility. **It's not about who gives you the most today — it's about who builds a better tomorrow.**

The Battle Cry: From Slaves to Leaders

We've been slaves to a corrupt system for too long. It's time to stop complaining and start acting. If they won't give us a seat at the table — we'll build a new table. If they won't listen — we'll speak louder. If they won't step aside — we'll push forward.

This isn't just a call for political involvement. It's a call for a revolution of the mind. To think. To question. To break free from the illusion that we are powerless.

Because we are not. We are the force that can reshape nations. The only question left is— **will you be part of the revolution, or will you let history repeat itself?**

The reins of this nation belong in our hands. The future belongs to those who dare to take it.

Will you be a slave — or will you rise?

The **<u>choice</u>** is yours.

Humanity Above All

Look around. What do you see? A world divided—not by walls of stone but by walls of the mind. Walls built on the fragile foundations of religion, caste, race, and nationality. We fight, argue, and even shed blood over identities that were meant to guide us, not divide us. And while we remain busy in these petty battles, those in power tighten their grip, smiling as we unknowingly play into their hands.

Is this what humanity has come to?

The Forgotten Truth: We Are One

Long before religions were established and borders were drawn, we were simply *human*. The first breath a child takes does not carry the stamp of religion or caste. The heart that beats within each of us does not pump blood based on nationality or sect. Pain feels the same, whether you're Hindu, Muslim, Christian, Sikh, or atheist. Joy lights up faces regardless of caste or creed.

So, if our birth and emotions are universal, why should our lives be any different?

The truth is stark and simple: Our first and foremost religion is humanity. Every other identity comes second.

Divided We Fall: Who Truly Benefits?

Think of history—the British *divide and rule* strategy. They didn't conquer nations by strength alone but by exploiting divisions among people. Sadly, the British are gone, but the strategy remains. Only now, it's our own politicians and power-seekers pulling the strings.

They ignite the fire of division, and we, like dry leaves, catch the flames without questioning. They throw slogans, manipulate emotions, and distort facts. And while we burn bridges with each other, they build their empires.

Who suffers? We do. *Who benefits?* They do.

It's tragic how easily we fall for the same trap, generation after generation, despite the lessons of history.

Education Without Wisdom Is Useless

We often believe that education will liberate us from ignorance. But what good is education if it doesn't teach us empathy? What is the value of intelligence if it fuels pride rather than compassion?

The most educated among us hold the greatest responsibility. It is not enough to secure degrees, earn wealth, and live in comfort. True education demands action—action against injustice, ignorance, and division.

If the educated remain silent while society tears itself apart, they become accomplices in the crime. As Martin Luther King Jr. once said, *"The ultimate tragedy is not the oppression and cruelty by the bad people but the silence over that by the good people."*

Humanity: The Only Religion That Truly Matters

Imagine a world where religion and caste do not define us. A world where a hungry child is fed without asking their background. Where a person in need receives help, no questions asked. Where love, kindness, and understanding form the core of every interaction.

It's not a utopian dream—it's entirely possible if we prioritize our shared humanity. Every religion, at its core, teaches compassion and brotherhood. Yet, we cling to superficial differences, forgetting the universal message:

- Hinduism: *"Vasudhaiva Kutumbakam" –World is one family.*
- Islam: *"To save one life is to save all of humanity."*
- Christianity: *"Love thy neighbor as thyself."*
- Sikhism: *"Recognize the entire human race as one."*
- Buddhism: *"Treat not others in ways that you yourself would find hurtful."*

If every faith preaches unity, why do its followers practice division?

A Plea for Change: Rise Above the Lies

It's time we ask ourselves:

- *Will I allow someone else to dictate whom I should love or hate?*
- *Will I judge a person by their character or their caste?*
- *Will I stand by while my community is manipulated into division?*

We must rise above the noise, question the narratives fed to us, and reject the politics of hatred. It starts with you—with one conversation, one act of kindness, one refusal to participate in divisive rhetoric.

Be the Change You Wish to See

Every great change in history began with individuals who refused to conform to ignorance.

- When Rosa Parks refused to give up her seat, she sparked the civil rights movement.
- When Mahatma Gandhi chose non-violence, he awakened a nation.
- When Malala Yousafzai stood for education, she inspired millions.

Change does not come from complaining about society. It comes from becoming the example society needs.

Be the person who bridges gaps, not one who widens them. Speak up when you witness discrimination. Teach children that no caste or religion defines worth. Choose love over hate, unity over division, and humanity over politics.

A Vision for the Future: One Humanity, One World

Imagine a future where children aren't taught to identify first by religion but by their shared humanity. Where leaders are chosen for their integrity, not their ability to exploit divisions. Where people unite not against each other but against poverty, injustice, and inequality.

This future is not a fantasy—it's a choice. A choice we can make every single day.

So, ask yourself:

- *Will I continue the cycle of division?*
- *Or will I break free, embrace humanity, and inspire others to do the same?*

Because in the end, we won't be remembered by our religion or caste but by the love we gave, the lives we touched, and the bridges we built.

Let us not be remembered as the generation that fought among ourselves. Let us be remembered as the generation that chose humanity.

Because when the power lies within you. Every word you speak, every action you take, either fuels division or fosters unity. Choose when dust settles, when borders fade and identities dissolve, only one truth remains:

We are human. And that is enough.

Making Life Meaningful

"A life lived for others is a life worthwhile." – **Albert Einstein**

This simple yet profound statement captures the essence of a meaningful life. In a world often obsessed with personal achievement, wealth, and recognition, it's easy to get trapped in the cycle of self-centred pursuits. Yet, when the applause fades and the possessions lose their charm, one question lingers: *"Did my life matter?"*

The answer lies not in what we accumulate but in how we uplift others. True fulfilment comes when we transcend the narrow confines of the self and embrace the interconnectedness of all beings. Let's explore how living for others gives life its deepest meaning.

Why Self-Centered Success Feels Hollow

Many chase success, believing it will bring happiness. They climb corporate ladders, amass wealth, and collect accolades, only to find an unsettling emptiness at the top. Why? Because self-centered achievements rarely nourish the soul.

Example: Howard Hughes, one of the wealthiest men of his time, died isolated and miserable despite his fortune. His riches couldn't replace the connection and purpose he lacked.

Philosopher **Jean-Paul Sartre** captured this existential void perfectly: *"Man is nothing else but what he makes of* *himself."* If we build a life solely around self-interest, it collapses under its own weight. Only when we contribute to others do we find true significance.

The Paradox of Happiness: Giving Is Receiving

Interestingly, the more we give, the richer we feel. Modern psychology supports what ancient wisdom always taught: altruism enhances well-being. Helping others releases oxytocin, the "love hormone," while reducing stress and boosting happiness.

Example: Studies show that volunteers live longer, healthier lives. Their generosity not only benefits others but also enriches their own existence.

As the Dalai Lama wisely said: *"If you want others to be happy, practice compassion. If you want to be happy, practice compassion."*

Thus, serving others isn't self-sacrifice—it's self-fulfilment.

The Ripple Effect of Kindness

Living for others doesn't always mean grand gestures. Small acts of kindness can transform lives, creating ripples that extend far beyond what we see.

- A teacher encouraging a struggling student can ignite lifelong confidence.
- A stranger's smile can brighten someone's dark day.
- A listening ear can ease the weight of silent suffering.

Example: Think of **Mother Teresa**, who didn't eradicate poverty but changed countless lives through simple acts of love. She believed: _"Not all of us can do great things. But we can do small things with great love."_

Even the tiniest act of selflessness plants seeds of hope in the world.

Why Living for Others Creates Meaning

Living for others gives life structure, direction, and emotional depth. It aligns us with something greater than fleeting pleasures. Here's why it matters:

- **Connection:** Human beings are wired for connection. When we help others, we reinforce the bonds that make life rich and resilient.
- **Purpose:** Knowing your actions ease someone's burden gives life clarity and motivation.
- **Legacy:** Material possessions fade, but the lives we touch form an eternal legacy.

Example: Think of **Mahatma Gandhi**. He didn't seek personal glory but fought for India's freedom through non-violence. His impact transcended generations, proving that service outlives the self.

Overcoming the Ego: The Spiritual Shift

To live for others, one must confront the ego—the voice that demands attention, superiority, and control.

The ego thrives on separation: *"Me vs. Them."* But the heart understands unity: *"We are one."*

Philosopher **Kahlil Gibran** beautifully wrote: _"You give but little when you give of your possessions. It is when you give of yourself that you truly give."_

This spiritual shift—from *"What can I take?"* to *"What can I give?"*—unlocks profound peace. It's not about denying yourself but expanding your sense of self to include others.

Practical Ways to Live for Others

Living selflessly doesn't mean abandoning your dreams or well-being. It means integrating service into daily life:

1. **Practice Active Listening:** Often, people don't need advice—they need to feel heard.
2. **Share Your Skills:** Whether it's teaching, mentoring, or creating, your talents can uplift others.
3. **Be Kind Daily:** A smile, a thank-you, or a helping hand can transform someone's day.
4. **Support Causes You Care About:** Volunteer, donate, or advocate for issues close to your heart.
5. **Be Present for Loved Ones:** Time and attention are the most precious gifts.

The Ultimate Realization: We Are All Connected

At its core, living for others reflects a deeper truth: *we are not separate.* The joy or pain of one affects the whole. Ancient spiritual traditions emphasize this unity:

- **Hinduism:** *"Atman (self) is Brahman (universal spirit)."*
- **Buddhism:** *"When you see others as yourself, compassion arises naturally."*
- **Christianity:** *"Love thy neighbour as thyself."*

Even modern science, through quantum physics, hints at an interconnected universe. Thus, serving others is not charity—it's self-realization.

What Truly Matters at the End?

Imagine you're at the end of your life, reflecting on your journey. Will you measure success by the wealth you amassed or the lives you touched?

As poet **Maya Angelou** said, _"I've learned that people will forget what you said, people will forget what you did, but people will never forget how you made them feel."_

In the final moments, what brings peace isn't personal gain but knowing you made the world a little brighter for someone else.

Conclusion: The Beauty of a Shared Life

Ultimately, life finds meaning not in isolation but in connection. By living for others, we escape the prison of the ego and embrace the vastness of shared humanity.

To paraphrase Einstein's wisdom: *"Only a life lived for others is a life worthwhile."*

Not because we must sacrifice ourselves, but because in lifting others, we rise together. In giving, we receive. In serving, we find peace. And in loving, we become whole.

So, ask yourself: *What legacy of kindness will I leave behind?* Because at the end of the journey, that's all that truly matters.

The True Purpose of Life: A Journey Within

Have you ever paused amid the chaos of life and asked yourself, *"Why am I here?"* It's a question that has haunted the minds of poets, philosophers, and common people alike. We chase success, love, recognition, and material comforts, only to realize that fulfilment often remains elusive. Why? Because purpose isn't found in the external world—it's discovered within.

The Myth of External Purpose

Society conditions us to believe that purpose lies in achieving milestones—earning a degree, securing a high-paying job, getting married, or buying a house. While these accomplishments bring temporary satisfaction, they rarely lead to lasting contentment.

Take the example of **Robin Williams**, a man who made the world laugh while battling his own inner turmoil. Despite fame and fortune, something profound was missing. His story reminds us that external achievements can't fill an internal void.

As the Bhagavad Gita wisely states: *"You have the right to perform your duties, but you are not entitled to the fruits of your actions."* This suggests that true purpose comes from the journey itself, not the destination.

Turning Inward: The Real Quest Begins

Finding purpose is less about *what you do* and more about *who you become*. It requires introspection, self-awareness, and a willingness to confront your deepest fears and desires. Here's how you can embark on this transformative journey:

A. Listen to Your Inner Voice

In the silence of solitude, the mind settles, and the heart speaks. Start by asking yourself:

- *What makes me lose track of time?*
- *What would I do even if I weren't paid for it?*
- *What kind of impact do I want to leave behind?*

Example: Steve Jobs once said, *"Have the courage to follow your heart and intuition. They somehow already know what you truly want to become."* His passion for innovation shaped not just his life but the world itself.

B. Embrace the Power of Service

Purpose often reveals itself when we transcend self-interest and contribute to something larger than ourselves. The most fulfilled individuals are those who uplift others.

Example: Mother Teresa didn't find her purpose in comfort but in serving the poor. Her life exemplifies how purpose flourishes when we shift from *"What can I gain?"* to *"How can I give?"*

C. Accept Impermanence and Live Authentically

Many search for purpose as though it's a fixed destination. But life is fluid, and so is purpose. What matters at 20 may not matter at 40. Embrace change and align your life with your evolving values.

The Buddha taught: *"The trouble is, you think you have time."* This profound truth reminds us to live authentically, without waiting for the "perfect moment."

What Truly Matters at the End?

Imagine you're at the twilight of your life. Will you measure success by the wealth you accumulated, the accolades you received, or the followers you gained? Or will it be the lives you touched, the love you shared, and the peace you found within?

Bronnie Ware, a nurse who spent years caring for dying patients, wrote a book titled *"The Top Five Regrets of the Dying."* The most common regret was: *"I wish I'd had the courage to live a life true to myself, not the life others expected of me."*

In the end, what truly matters is:

- **Inner Peace:** Did you find joy in the present moment?
- **Meaningful Connections:** Did you love and let yourself be loved?
- **Authentic Living:** Did you honour your true self?
- **Positive Impact:** Did you leave the world a little better than you found it?

A Simple Path to Purpose: The Ikigai Model

The Japanese concept of *Ikigai* (生き甲斐) beautifully captures the essence of purpose. It lies at the intersection of four things:

1. **What you love (Passion)**
2. **What you are good at (Profession)**
3. **What the world needs (Mission)**
4. **What you can be paid for (Vocation)**

Reflecting on these areas can illuminate a path that feels both fulfilling and sustainable.

Final Thoughts: The Journey Is the Purpose

Rumi, the great Persian poet, once wrote: _"When the soul lies down in that grass, the world is too full to talk about. Ideas, language—even the phrase each other—do not make any sense."_

Purpose isn't found in a single moment of revelation but in the continuous unfolding of life itself. It's in the books you read, the smiles you share, the risks you take, and the quiet moments of gratitude.

So, stop chasing purpose as if it's a treasure hidden at the end of a map. Instead, live mindfully, love deeply, serve passionately, and embrace each moment. In doing so, you'll realize that *life itself is the purpose*, and everything else is just noise.

The Education System: From Factories of Obedience to Foundries of Humanity

Our education system — once a beacon of knowledge and enlightenment — has devolved into a soul-crushing factory, mass-producing robots instead of raising free-thinking, compassionate human beings. It has forgotten its roots, its purpose, and its responsibility. The very institutions meant to awaken young minds have become prisons that silence creativity, punish curiosity, and reward blind obedience. And the worst part? We accept it. We call it 'normal.'

But what if this 'normal' is the problem?

The Roots We Abandoned

Education wasn't always like this. Once upon a time, it was about self-discovery, about nurturing the mind and soul. The ancient Indian Gurukul system didn't teach students to memorize answers — it taught them how to *ask questions.* It wasn't about producing labourers for an economy; it was about producing leaders, philosophers, warriors, and artists — individuals capable of shaping the world, not just surviving in it.

Fast forward to today. What do we have? A system designed by the British colonialists to create clerks and obedient workers — and we never updated it. The chains are still there, just painted in brighter colours.

What We Call 'Education' Is Brainwashing

From the moment a child steps into school, they're shoved into an assembly line:

- **Memorize, don't understand.**
- **Obey, don't question.**
- **Compete, don't collaborate.**
- **Conform, don't create.**

We measure intelligence by how well students can cram information, regurgitate it in exams, and forget it the next day. Critical thinking? Irrelevant. Emotional intelligence? Ignored. Practical skills? Who cares? As long as you score well, you're a 'good student.'

This is not education. This is programming.

The Coaching Epidemic: Education for Sale

The rise of coaching institutes is a direct consequence of this broken system. These centres have become pressure cookers where students are cooked alive, chasing a mirage of 'guaranteed success.' Parents pour their life savings into these institutes, believing the promises of a 'bright future.' But what they often get is a child drowning in anxiety, depression, and hopelessness.

The coaching industry thrives on one thing: fear. Fear of failure, fear of poverty, fear of disappointing family and society. They sell hope — but what they really deliver is burnout.

The Human Cost: Anxiety, Depression, Suicide

Let's stop pretending. This system isn't just flawed— it's killing our youth.

Anxiety attacks, depression, and suicides have become alarmingly common among students. They're not scared of exams, they're scared of what happens if they fail. Because in this system, failure isn't a lesson; it's a life sentence. Students who dare to dream beyond engineering, medicine, or government jobs are labelled 'failures' by their families and society.

The truth is, they're not failing — the system is.

The Purpose of Education: A Lost Philosophy

What is the true purpose of education? Is it to memorize textbooks, get a degree, and secure a job that pays enough to survive? Or is it to create individuals who can think, question, innovate, and feel empathy for others?

Education is More Than Just a degree

In an era where academic qualifications often dictate societal status, it is crucial to acknowledge that real education is not confined to diplomas or prestigious institutions. As Shakuntala Devi insightfully stated, *"Education is not just about going to school and getting a degree. It's about widening your knowledge and absorbing the truth about life."*

Many individuals with impressive degrees lack critical thinking, empathy, or ethical integrity—qualities that define an educated mind. On the other hand, there are people without formal education who possess immense wisdom, life experience, and an ability to solve real-world problems. True education empowers individuals to think independently, question assumptions, and embrace lifelong learning.

Education—A Journey, Not Just a Destination

Education has long been perceived as a means to secure a job, earn a stable income, and achieve professional success. However, true education extends far beyond the confines of classrooms and textbooks. It is about shaping intellect, nurturing character, and fostering a lifelong quest for knowledge. Martin Luther King Jr. wisely said, *"The function of education is to teach one to think intensively and to think critically. Intelligence plus character—that is the goal of true education."* This statement serves as a guiding principle in understanding what education truly means.

Education is not merely about financial success or professional achievement—it is about living a meaningful and purposeful life. Brad Henry captures this essence, saying, *"Education is not solely about earning a great living. It means living a great life."* A truly educated person understands the importance of ethics, moral responsibility, and compassion.

Consider the example of Mahatma Gandhi, who was a lawyer by profession but used his knowledge for the greater good of society. His education was not just about acquiring legal expertise; it was about applying wisdom and character to lead a movement for justice and equality. Similarly, figures like Nelson Mandela and Mother Teresa exemplify the power of education when it is driven by a higher purpose rather than personal gain.

The purpose of education is **liberation** — mental, emotional, and spiritual. It's meant to create free minds, not obedient slaves. It's meant to empower, not suppress. Education should teach us how to live, not just how to earn.

As the philosopher Jiddu Krishnamurti once said, *"It is no measure of health to be well adjusted to a profoundly sick society."*

Our education system rewards adjustment. It punishes those who rebel, those who think differently, and those who refuse to play by the rules. But it's the rebels, the thinkers, the creators — the misfits — who change the world.

Critical Thinking: The Heart of True Education

One of the fundamental aspects of education is the ability to think critically. A society that lacks critical thinking fosters ignorance, blind conformity, and manipulation. Education should encourage questioning, analysis, and the courage to challenge outdated norms.

Today, with the proliferation of misinformation and fake news, the need for an education system that promotes independent thought is greater than ever. The ability to discern truth from falsehood, analyse situations objectively, and make informed decisions is a direct result of a well-rounded education.

Education and Emotional Intelligence

A person may have immense academic knowledge but fail to navigate human relationships with understanding and compassion. True education must integrate emotional intelligence, teaching individuals how to manage emotions, empathize with others, and develop meaningful relationships.

Workplaces, societies, and governments thrive not just on intellectual acumen but also on emotional intelligence. Leaders who lack empathy and ethical judgment can cause irreparable damage to societies, regardless of their academic credentials.

Education as a Tool for Social Change

Education is a powerful force in transforming societies. It eradicates poverty, promotes gender equality, and empowers marginalized communities. An educated society is a progressive society, where individuals are aware of their rights, responsibilities, and the value of democratic participation.

Nations that prioritize holistic education have witnessed remarkable progress. For instance, Finland's education system is renowned for fostering creativity, critical thinking, and personal growth rather than rote learning and exam scores. As a result, it has one of the highest literacy rates and overall well-being indexes in the world.

What We Need: A Revolution in Education

We don't need another reform. We need a **revolution.**

- **Replace rote learning with critical thinking.** Students should be taught how to think, not what to think.

- **Prioritize emotional intelligence and empathy.** A society full of intellectuals without humanity is a dangerous one.

- **Teach practical life skills.** Taxes, laws, mental health, communication, and creativity — these should be core subjects.

- **Destroy the obsession with grades.** A number on a piece of paper does not define a human being's worth.
- **Redefine success.** Teach students that success isn't about wealth or status — it's about finding purpose and making a difference.

The Final Call: We Are Not Machines

We are humans — not robots. We're not here to memorize, obey, and die. We're here to create, love, and leave this world better than we found it.

The question is — will you let this broken system define who you are? Will you let them turn you into a lifeless cog in their machine? Or will you rise, unlearn their lies, and reclaim the true purpose of education — to become the best, most authentic version of yourself?

The future belongs to those who dare to think. Are you one of them?

It's time to stop surviving. It's time to start living. It's time to **wake up.**

Build a legacy, not just a resume

"Strive not to be a success, but rather to be of value." – Albert Einstein

In a world obsessed with accolades, wealth, and recognition, this timeless quote by Einstein serves as a gentle yet profound reminder: true greatness lies not in what we achieve for ourselves but in what we contribute to the world around us. Success, while alluring, is often fleeting. Value, however, creates an enduring legacy—it touches lives, inspires change, and defines character.

The Illusion of Success vs. The Power of Value

Success, as society defines it, is often measured by material accomplishments—high-paying jobs, luxury possessions, prestigious titles, and widespread fame. While these achievements can bring comfort and pride, they rarely offer lasting fulfilment. History is filled with stories of successful individuals who, despite their external triumphs, felt an inner void.

Take Howard Hughes, for example. Once the world's richest man, he lived in isolation during his final years, haunted by anxiety and dissatisfaction. Contrast this with someone like Mother Teresa, who owned little but lived a life of immense fulfilment by serving others. Her value to society far outweighed any material success she could have pursued.

Thus, the true measure of a person's worth lies not in their bank balance but in their character, compassion, and contributions. Value creates a ripple effect—when you enrich the lives of others, your legacy continues long after worldly successes fade.

Few Real-Life Examples: Value Over Success

Mahatma Gandhi: Gandhi could have pursued personal success as a lawyer, but he chose to live by the values of non-violence and truth, inspiring millions worldwide to fight injustice peacefully.

Mother Teresa: She did not seek fame or fortune. Instead, she dedicated her life to serving the poor and sick, becoming a global symbol of compassion and selflessness.

Dr. APJ Abdul Kalam: Known as the "Missile Man of India," Dr. Kalam never chased personal success. Instead, he dedicated his life to science, education, and inspiring the youth. His humility and commitment to uplifting others made him a beloved figure worldwide.

Ratan Tata: Unlike many industrialists who chase profits, Ratan Tata prioritized philanthropy, ethical business practices, and national development. His commitment to uplifting society through initiatives in education, healthcare, and rural development exemplifies true value.

Swami Vivekananda: Vivekananda did not seek personal fame but worked tirelessly to spread the message of spirituality, selflessness, and humanism. His teachings continue to inspire millions around the world.

Malala Yousafzai: Malala's fight for girls' education, even after surviving an assassination attempt, shows her dedication to creating value for society. Her advocacy has empowered countless young girls to pursue education.

Florence Nightingale: Known as the founder of modern nursing, Nightingale chose to serve the wounded rather than seek personal glory. Her contributions revolutionized healthcare worldwide.

Jane Goodall: As a primatologist and conservationist, Goodall didn't seek fame. Her lifelong dedication to wildlife conservation and advocacy for environmental sustainability turned her into an icon of positive change.

These individuals remind us that success can fade, but the value we create lives on.

Core Values to Inculcate for a Meaningful Life

To become a person of value, one must cultivate certain principles that shape character and guide actions. Here are ten such values worth embracing:

1. **Integrity:** *"Integrity is doing the right thing, even when no one is watching."* – C.S. Lewis Integrity means being honest and true to your principles. People trust those who stand by their word, regardless of circumstances.

2. **Empathy:** Understanding and sharing the feelings of others creates stronger connections. Empathy allows us to uplift those around us and build meaningful relationships.

3. **Humility:** A humble person acknowledges their strengths without arrogance and recognizes the contributions of others. The true value lies in lifting others, not in self-promotion.

4. **Respect:** Treating others with dignity, regardless of status or background, reflects one's character. Respect fosters harmony and mutual growth.

5. **Responsibility:** Taking ownership of one's actions, both successes and mistakes, builds resilience and earns respect. Responsible individuals contribute positively to society.

6. **Kindness:** Small acts of kindness create a significant impact. A kind word or gesture can brighten someone's day and inspire them to pay it forward.

7. **Perseverance:** Challenges are inevitable, but persistence transforms obstacles into opportunities. Perseverance reflects the commitment to personal growth and meaningful contributions.

8. **Generosity:** Sharing knowledge, time, or resources without expecting anything in return enriches both the giver and the receiver.

9. **Curiosity:** Lifelong learners remain adaptable and innovative. Curiosity drives self-improvement and opens doors to new opportunities.

10. **Gratitude:** Appreciating what we have fosters contentment and encourages us to give back to the world.

How to Become a Person of Value: A Step-by-Step Guide

1. **Define Your Purpose:** Identify what truly matters to you—whether it's helping others, creating art, or advancing knowledge—and align your actions accordingly.

2. **Practice Self-Awareness:** Reflect on your strengths, weaknesses, and motivations. This clarity helps you stay true to your values.

3. **Prioritize Service Over Self-Interest:** Look for ways to contribute—mentor someone, volunteer, or simply offer support to a friend in need.

4. **Build Meaningful Relationships:** Surround yourself with people who inspire and challenge you to grow.

5. **Lead by Example:** Demonstrate the values you wish to see in others. Actions often speak louder than words.

6. **Embrace Failure as a Teacher:** View setbacks not as defeats but as opportunities for growth and learning.

7. **Stay Grounded:** Success can be intoxicating, but staying humble ensures that your focus remains on creating value rather than accumulating accolades.

8. **Practice Daily Kindness:** Even small gestures—a smile, a kind word, or a helping hand—can create lasting impact.

9. **Commit to Lifelong Learning:** The more you grow, the more you can contribute to the world.

10. **Leave a Legacy:** Ask yourself: *How will people remember me?* Let your actions today shape the answer.

Final Thoughts: The Legacy of Value

In the grand narrative of life, success is but a fleeting chapter—what truly endures is the impact we leave behind. As Maya Angelou beautifully put it:

"People will forget what you said, people will forget what you did, but people will never forget how you made them feel."

So, strive not merely to climb the ladder of success but to build bridges of value along the way. In doing so, you will not only enrich your own life but also inspire countless others—a legacy far more meaningful than any material achievement.

Ultimately, the world needs more people who measure their worth not by what they have but by what they give. Will you be one of them?

The **choice** is yours.

The Best Way to Predict the Future of a Nation is by Looking at Its Youth

Dr. A.P.J. Abdul Kalam, the former president of India and one of the greatest visionaries of our time, once said, *"The best way to predict the future of a nation is by looking at its youth."* This statement holds profound significance, as the youth are not just the inheritors of a nation's past but the architects of its future. The strength, vision, and values they uphold today will shape the destiny of their country tomorrow.

In every great civilization, from the Renaissance to the modern digital era, it has been the young minds that have driven progress and innovation. But for youth to be the real game-changers, they must first realize who they are for the nation, what they can do, and how they can contribute effectively.

Who is the Youth for the Nation?

Youth are often called the backbone of a nation because they bring energy, creativity, and fresh perspectives. They are the driving force of social, economic, and technological change. But their role is not just limited to building careers and businesses; they hold the responsibility of shaping a just, progressive, and sustainable society.

Characteristics of the Youth That Make Them Crucial for Nation-Building:

- **Energy & Enthusiasm:** The ability to work tirelessly, adapt quickly, and drive change.

- **Innovative Thinking:** A capacity to think outside the box and find solutions to national and global problems.
- **Resilience & Courage:** The strength to challenge outdated norms and push for reforms.
- **Moral Responsibility:** The power to uphold and spread ethical values, integrity, and justice.
- **Social Awareness:** The sensitivity to recognize social problems and actively work towards solutions.

Mahatma Gandhi believed in the power of youth, stating, *"The future depends on what you do today."* If today's youth invest in education, integrity, and action, the future of the nation will be bright.

What Can the Youth Do for Their Country?

Understanding their potential, youth must engage in meaningful actions to transform their nation. Here are some key areas where they can contribute:

1. Lead Social Change and Upliftment

Young people have always been at the forefront of revolutions. Be it the Indian independence movement, the Civil Rights Movement in the U.S., or modern climate activism, it is the youth who have led the charge.

- Fight against corruption, inequality, and discrimination.
- Work towards gender equality and social justice.
- Actively engage in volunteerism and social work.

2. Drive Innovation and Economic Growth

Nations that thrive economically have strong entrepreneurial youth.

- Start businesses that create jobs and boost the economy.
- Innovate in science, technology, and digital transformation.
- Support 'Make in India' and similar initiatives to strengthen the nation's industries.

3. Strengthen Democracy and Governance

For a country to progress, its democratic institutions must be strong.

- Participate in voting and encourage informed electoral decisions.
- Question and hold leaders accountable for governance.
- Join civil services, law enforcement, or policymaking roles to drive change from within.

4. Protect and Preserve the Environment

Sustainable development is critical for a nation's future.

- Reduce waste, conserve energy, and promote eco-friendly lifestyles.
- Join global efforts to combat climate change.
- Innovate sustainable technologies and advocate for green policies.

5. Advance Education and Skill Development

An educated youth leads to a prosperous nation.

- Promote literacy programs and mentor underprivileged students.
- Develop skills in science, mathematics, technology, and arts to contribute effectively to global advancements.
- Support research and development in areas critical for national progress.

How Can Youth Achieve This?

It is not enough to have the desire to change the nation; youth must take concrete steps to bring about transformation.

1. Self-Improvement and Knowledge Building

The first step towards contributing to the nation is self-growth.

- Read books and articles, and stay informed about current events.
- Gain expertise in a chosen field and excel in it.
- Develop emotional intelligence and leadership skills.

2. Be Proactive and Take Initiative

- Participate in leadership programs, community projects, and innovation hubs.
- Create startups or organizations that address national challenges.

- Take part in social movements, policy discussions, and volunteer programs.

3. Collaborate and Build Networks

- Join youth organizations that work for social change.
- Engage with mentors and role models who can guide them.
- Work together beyond regional, religious, and class barriers to create unity and strength.

4. Develop a Strong Moral Compass

As Swami Vivekananda famously said, *"Give me 100 energetic young men and I shall transform India."* The youth must uphold strong moral values, act with integrity, and ensure that they lead by example.

5. Overcome Challenges with Resilience

There will be obstacles on the path, but a determined youth can overcome them.

- Stay motivated despite failures.
- Learn from mistakes and keep moving forward.
- Push back against negative influences and stay true to national values.

Conclusion: The Time Is Now!

Youth are not just the future; they are the present force that can redefine the nation's destiny. A nation's prosperity, global standing, and social fabric depend on how well its youth rise to the occasion.

As Dr. A.P.J. Abdul Kalam rightly said, *"Dream, dream, dream. Dreams transform into thoughts and thoughts result in action."* The youth must dream of a better future, think of innovative ways to achieve it, and act with determination.

The time to wait is over. The time to act is now. The question is no longer, *"What will our country do for us?"* but rather, *"What can we, the youth, do for our country?"* The answer lies in self-improvement, proactive engagement, and a relentless pursuit of excellence. The future of our nation is in the hands of its youth, and they must rise to the challenge!

Let us pledge to be the change-makers who will transform our nation into a beacon of progress, justice, and prosperity.

The Choice: The Unseen Power Shaping Your Life

Life is nothing more than a series of choices — each one a fork in the road that determines who we become. Some choices are small and seemingly insignificant, while others shape entire destinies. But what if I told you that one wrong choice, one impulsive decision, could ripple through generations, altering not only your life but the lives of countless others? This is the silent, unstoppable force of **The Choice**.

The Illusion of Control

We live under the comforting illusion that we control everything — our lives, our outcomes, our futures. But the truth is, we only control one thing: our choices. Once a decision is made, the consequences are no longer in our hands. Like a stone thrown into a still lake, the ripples expand beyond what we can see.

Imagine standing at the edge of a vast ocean. Each wave is a choice you've made. Some waves are gentle, barely reaching the shore. Others rise like tsunamis, reshaping the landscape entirely. You may not see the full force of your decisions immediately — but they always leave a mark.

The Domino Effect of a Single Decision

Picture a line of dominoes stretching to the horizon. The first tile is small, innocent even. One push, one bad choice, and the chain reaction begins. A lie told to avoid trouble leads to more lies, each one heavier than the last. A moment of anger escalates into violence. One decision to follow the crowd leads to years of regret.

Let's make this real. A teenager, pressured by friends, takes part in a robbery. It seems like a quick way to get money — a momentary thrill. But that decision doesn't end when the money is spent. Someone gets hurt. A life is lost. Families are broken. The teen is caught and imprisoned. Their future — once full of potential — is now a cautionary tale. One night, one choice, and lives are permanently shattered.

The Weight of Regret

Regret is a prison of its own kind, and the bars are made of our past decisions. People often say, "I wish I could go back and change things." But time is merciless. It moves forward, never back.

Imagine carrying a backpack filled with bricks. Each brick is a bad choice. At first, the weight feels manageable. But with every wrong decision, another brick is added. Eventually, the weight becomes unbearable. You sink under the pressure of what you could have done differently.

The harsh reality is that regret doesn't change the past. It only reminds us of what we've lost — opportunities missed, relationships broken, potential wasted.

The Legacy of a Choice

When you make a decision, you're not just affecting your life — you're influencing the lives of everyone around you. A father who abandons his family leaves scars on his children that may never heal. A young person who turns to crime leaves behind grieving parents and shattered dreams.

But the same power works in reverse. A student who chooses to study instead of party might inspire their younger sibling to value education. A person who breaks free from addiction shows their friends that change is possible. A teenager who stands up to a bully could empower others to do the same.

Your choices don't just shape you. They create a legacy — one that will outlive you.

Choosing a Different Path

So, what do you do when you're standing at that fork in the road? How do you ensure you make the right choice, the one that leads to growth, not destruction?

1. **Pause and Reflect** – Before making a decision, stop. Ask yourself, "Will this move me closer to the person I want to become, or push me further away?"

2. **Own Your Choices** – Don't let others decide for you. Following the crowd is easy — but it rarely leads to greatness. Be brave enough to think for yourself.

3. **Consider the Ripples** – Visualize the long-term consequences. Who might this decision hurt? Who might it help? Will you be proud of this choice years from now?

4. **Seek Wisdom** – Talk to people who have walked the path before you. Learn from their successes — and their mistakes.

5. **Make the Hard Choice** – Sometimes, the right decision is the hardest one. It takes strength to walk away from the easy path when you know it leads to a dead end.

The Choice Is Yours — Always Has Been

In the end, everything boils down to one truth: **You are the author of your own story.** Each decision you make writes a new line, a new chapter. Will your story be one of regret or redemption? Of wasted potential or unstoppable growth? Of selfishness or selflessness?

The choice is — and always will be — yours.

And remember this: even if you've made bad choices before, it's never too late to start making better ones. The next chapter is unwritten. Make it one worth reading.

Togetherness: The Power of Unity

In a world that often glorifies individual success, we tend to overlook an essential truth: no one truly thrives alone. Togetherness is the invisible thread that holds humanity together, transforming isolated dreams into shared realities. As the iconic quote goes, *"A dream you dream alone is only a dream. A dream you dream together is reality."* This isn't just poetic wisdom — it's a blueprint for achieving the extraordinary.

The Strength in Unity

Humans are social beings. From the earliest days of civilization, survival wasn't about the strongest individual but the most connected community. Alone, we are limited by our own knowledge, skills, and endurance. Together, we combine our strengths, balance our weaknesses, and uplift one another.

Imagine a single stick. It's easy to break. But bind several sticks together, and they become unbreakable. This metaphor isn't just about physical strength — it's about emotional resilience, mental fortitude, and the unstoppable force that emerges when people work in harmony.

Dreams Realized Through Togetherness

John Lennon's words, *"A dream you dream alone is only a dream. A dream you dream together is reality,"* highlighting an essential principle: shared vision amplifies potential. Think of history's greatest movements — from civil rights to technological revolutions. They weren't powered by one person's desire but by a collective belief that change was possible.

Take India's fight for independence. It wasn't the dream of one individual but a united struggle led by countless brave souls, inspired by a shared vision of freedom. Mahatma Gandhi didn't walk alone; he walked with millions. Together, they turned an impossible dream into an undeniable reality.

Where There's a Will, There's a Way — Together

The proverb *"Where there's a will, there's a way"* takes on even greater strength when paired with togetherness. A lone will can falter, lose hope, or face obstacles too large to overcome. But a collective will — united by purpose — becomes an unstoppable force.

Consider the moon landing. It wasn't the achievement of one brilliant mind but of thousands of scientists, engineers, and dreamers working in unison. Their shared determination propelled humanity beyond earthly limits.

The Emotional Power of Togetherness

Beyond achievements and goals, togetherness fulfills a deeper human need: connection. It gives us a sense of belonging, a reminder that we are not alone in our struggles. When we stand together, burdens feel lighter, and joy feels richer.

Think about moments of personal hardship. A comforting word from a friend or a family member's unwavering support can turn despair into hope. Togetherness isn't just about achieving great things — it's about enduring life's storms with the strength of a collective heart.

Building a Future Together

So, how can we embrace and foster togetherness?

- **Listen and empathize:** True togetherness begins with understanding. By listening to others' perspectives and empathizing with their experiences, we create genuine connections.

- **Collaborate, don't compete:** The mindset of *"us versus them"* divides. But collaboration breeds innovation and unity.

- **Celebrate each other's victories:** One person's success doesn't diminish another's worth. When we celebrate each other, we foster an environment where everyone thrives.

- **Stand together in adversity:** It's easy to unite during success, but true togetherness is proven during hardship. Be the pillar for others, and you'll find they become yours when you need them most.

The Legacy of Togetherness

Togetherness isn't just a strategy for success — it's a legacy we leave behind. When we uplift others, we create a ripple effect that inspires future generations. *"Each one, teach one."* The wisdom, kindness, and strength we share today shape the world tomorrow.

Let's not fall into the illusion of solitary greatness. Let's recognize the power that lies in standing together. After all, a single star may shine brightly, but a sky full of stars illuminates the entire night.

So, ask yourself: Who are you standing with? And who are you inviting to stand with you? Because together, we can turn dreams into reality — and make the impossible possible.

Clarity: The Foundation of Peak Performance

Imagine standing at the edge of a dense forest, fog rolling thick between the trees. You know there's a beautiful destination on the other side — a place of success, fulfilment, and happiness — but without a clear path, you wander aimlessly. This is what life looks like without clarity.

Clarity is the sunlight that burns through the fog, revealing the path forward. It's the compass that aligns your heart, mind, and actions. In the pursuit of any great achievement, whether personal or professional, clarity is the bedrock upon which peak performance is built. Let's dive into this essential principle by exploring vision, mission, and goals — the three pillars that define clarity.

The Power of Goals: Why Success Follows Those with a Clear Direction

Why are some people wildly successful while others seem stuck, drifting from one thing to another? The answer often boils down to a single concept: having a clear, defined goal. People with goals are successful because they know exactly where they're going — and that clarity fuels their journey.

Let's explore this through a powerful analogy that perfectly illustrates why having a goal isn't optional — it's essential.

The Ship Analogy: Success with a Map

Imagine a ship about to leave port. It has a captain, a trained crew, and a detailed map outlining the entire journey. The destination is clear, and everyone on board knows the route and the time it will take to get there. This ship is destined for success — it will reach its destination 999 times out of 1000 missions. It's practically guaranteed.

The ship's success isn't a fluke. It's a result of having a clear goal, a plan, and a team working towards that outcome. This is how success works in life, too — when you know where you're headed, you dramatically increase your chances of getting there.

Now picture a second ship, identical in structure but completely different in its approach. This one has no captain, no crew, no map, and no defined destination. It's set adrift with no guidance or purpose. What happens to this ship? It's painfully obvious: it will either sink, get caught in a storm, or end up stranded on some deserted island. Reaching a meaningful destination isn't even a possibility.

Isn't this how life works, too? Without goals, we're like that rudderless ship — drifting aimlessly, vulnerable to the tides and storms of life. Success isn't random. It requires purpose, direction, and deliberate action.

The Ultimate Secret: You Become What You Think

Now, let's uncover the most powerful truth of all — a truth so simple yet profound that it has echoed through history.

We become what we think.

Every great thinker, philosopher, and leader in history, despite their differences, agreed on this one thing. Your dominant thoughts shape your reality. If you think like a winner — setting clear goals, believing in yourself, and taking consistent action — you'll achieve success. If your mind is clouded with fear, doubt, and aimlessness, you'll get stuck in that reality instead.

This is more than motivation — it's a universal law of human success.

The Power of Vision, Mission, and Goals"

Vision: The "Why" — Your Ultimate Destination

The **vision** is your **big-picture dream** — where you want to **end up**. It's about **inspiration** and **purpose**.

It answers:

- **Why do we exist?**
- **What impact do we want to make in the long run?**

Example:

- **Tesla's Vision:** *"To create a sustainable future for energy."*
- **My Book's Vision:** *"To awaken the youth to break free from mental slavery and create a world driven by purpose, courage, and truth."*

Think of the vision like a **North Star** — you may never fully reach it, but it **guides every step** you take.

---

2. Mission: The "How" — Your Roadmap

The **mission** is about **action**. It explains **how** you're going to **turn your vision into reality** — the **methods, approaches, and mindset** you'll use to get there.

It answers:

- **What do we do?**
- **Who do we serve?**
- **How do we make a difference?**

Example:

- **Nike's Mission:** *"To bring inspiration and innovation to every athlete in the world." (And they add, "If you have a body, you're an athlete.")*
- **My Book's Mission:** *"To ignite a revolution in young minds by dismantling false beliefs, challenging corrupt systems, and empowering them to lead with wisdom, courage, and compassion."*

The mission is like the **engine** driving the journey.

---

3. Goals: The "What"— Your Milestones

Goals are **specific, measurable achievements** that bring the mission to life. They're **practical steps** — think of them as **checkpoints** on the road to your vision.

It answers:

- **What are the key achievements that'll prove we're succeeding?**
- **How do we measure progress?**

Example:

- **Google's Goal:** *"Organize the world's information and make it universally accessible and useful."*
- **My Book's Goals:**
  - *Reach and inspire 1 million young readers within 2 years.*

Goals should be **concrete, realistic, and time-bound** — like a **battle plan**.

When you align your vision, mission, and goals, you create an unstoppable force. Here's what happens:

- **Clarity:** You stop wasting energy on things that don't serve your purpose.
- **Focus:** You make better decisions because you know exactly what you're working towards.
- **Resilience:** When challenges hit (and they will), your vision keeps you going.
- **Fulfilment:** Success becomes more meaningful because you're building something bigger than yourself.

Most people wake up, go through the motions, and hope life gets better someday. Leaders — the ones who change the world — have a **vision**, a **mission**, and **goals** to guide them.

Why Clarity Fuels Peak Performance

Without clarity, you waste time, energy, and focus chasing distractions. It's like running on a treadmill — you're moving, but you're not getting anywhere. Clarity stops you from mistaking busyness for progress.

Here's a metaphor: Imagine an archer in a competition. Without a clear target, he can draw his bow and fire all day, but every shot is meaningless. The moment you place a bullseye in front of him, his focus sharpens. His muscles tense with purpose. His breathing slows. He's no longer just shooting arrows — he's aiming to win.

Clarity eliminates doubt, fuels confidence, and channels effort into meaningful action. It's the foundation of peak performance because it prevents wasted effort and ensures every move serves a higher purpose.

How to Cultivate Unstoppable Clarity

1. **Reflect Deeply:** Ask yourself what you truly want from life. What excites you? What legacy do you want to leave?

2. **Define Your Vision:** Craft a compelling, personal vision statement. Let it inspire and guide you.

3. **Create a Powerful Mission:** Determine how you'll live out that vision — the daily, consistent work you're willing to embrace.

4. **Set Specific Goals:** Break your mission into achievable, measurable steps. Review and adjust them regularly.

5. **Eliminate Distractions:** Anything that doesn't align with your vision is a detour. Learn to say no to distractions that dilute your focus.

Final Thought: The Power of Clarity

Clarity is the foundation on which greatness is built. With a clear vision, mission, and goals, you're no longer wandering through life — you're moving with intention, purpose, and unstoppable momentum.

Remember this: a lion chasing two gazelles catches none. Focus your energy on what truly matters to you. Once you're clear on your path, no obstacle, setback, or failure can derail you.

The lesson is clear: people with goals succeed because they know where they're going. Without goals, life becomes a directionless drift, leaving you vulnerable to failure and mediocrity.

So, ask yourself:

- Do you have a clear, compelling goal?
- Do you have a plan to reach it?
- Are you committed to pursuing it every day, no matter what obstacles arise?

If you embrace this mindset — if you truly believe that you become what you think — your life will transform. You'll no longer drift. You'll navigate, pursue, and achieve the success you've always dreamed of.

The choice is yours: set a goal, or let life set one for you.

Civic Sense: The Backbone of a Thriving Society

The Invisible Pillar of Civilization

Imagine walking through a park where the grass is vibrant, pathways are spotless, and the air smells fresh — only to turn a corner and find heaps of litter, vandalized walls, and blaring horns from a traffic jam caused by someone parking illegally. This stark contrast reveals a harsh reality: civic sense is the invisible force that defines whether a society thrives or deteriorates.

What is Civic Sense?

Civic sense is the awareness and practice of duties and responsibilities toward society. It embodies respect for laws, empathy for others, cleanliness, public order, and environmental consciousness.

Civic sense is more than a set of rules — it's an attitude, it's a way of life — a commitment to respecting public spaces and other citizens. Moral behaviour goes deeper, encompassing integrity, empathy, and a sense of responsibility toward the greater good.

To simplify it:

- **Civic sense** is the hand that throws garbage in the bin.
- **Moral behaviour** is the heart that feels bad for those who clean up after you.

Philosopher John Stuart Mill once said, *"The worth of a state, in the long run, is the worth of the individuals composing it."* If we want a better India, we must first become better individuals.

A Checklist of Civic Sense

Here's a breakdown of key civic responsibilities — a cheat sheet to being a responsible citizen:

- **Respect Public Property:** No spitting, urinating, or vandalizing walls.
- **Follow Traffic Rules:** Lane discipline, no honking, yield to pedestrians, and make way for ambulances.
- **Proper Waste Disposal:** Use dustbins, segregate waste, avoid plastic, and stop burning trash.
- **Respect Queues:** At bus stops, ticket counters, and anywhere. No cutting lines.
- **Maintain Noise Discipline:** Avoid blaring music in public spaces.
- **Be Punctual:** Value your time — and others'.
- **Avoid Corruption:** Say no to bribes, whether giving or taking.
- **Promote Inclusivity:** No discrimination based on caste, religion, or gender.
- **Pay Taxes Honestly:** It fuels the nation's infrastructure.
- **Protect Natural Resources:** Save water, plant trees, and avoid pollution.

Why Do We Lack Civic Sense?

Let's confront the uncomfortable truth. Why do we behave so poorly in public spaces? Here are four hard-hitting reasons:

1. **Faulty Socialization:** We're pampered at home—moms and maids clean up after us. We grow up expecting someone else to handle the mess.
2. **Flawed Education:** Our schools focus on rote learning, not citizenship. Civic sense isn't taught; it's assumed.
3. **Inequality and Hierarchy:** Caste, class, and wealth create divisions. We don't see public spaces as *ours* — just someone else's problem.
4. **Low Expectations:** We've normalized filth and chaos. If we expect squalor, that's what we'll get.

Why is Civic Sense Important?

The quality of life in any country hinges on the civic sense of its citizens. Let's break this down:

1. **Health and Hygiene:** Clean streets and public places reduce the spread of diseases.
2. **Safety and Order**: Following traffic rules and respecting others prevents accidents and chaos.
3. **Economic Growth:** A well-maintained, organized environment attracts tourism, investments, and global opportunities.
4. **Social Harmony:** Respect for others, irrespective of religion, caste, or gender, fosters unity and peace.

5. **Environmental Sustainability:** Conserving resources, reducing pollution, and protecting nature ensure a liveable future.

The 4 Es of Change: Educate, Engineer, Enforce, Engage

Let's not drown in despair. Here's a blueprint for change — the **4 Es**:

1. **Educate:** Start young. Schools should teach civic responsibility, environmental awareness, and moral values — not through textbooks but through hands-on, participatory learning. Parents must lead by example.

2. **Engineer:** Better urban design encourages better behaviour. Think clean, accessible public toilets, abundant dustbins, clear road signage, and reliable public transport — like the Delhi Metro.

3. **Enforce:** Without penalties, rules are suggestions. We need more 'Safai Marshals' — on-the-spot fines for littering, urinating in public, or breaking traffic laws.

4. **Engage:** Citizen activism can't be optional. Join movements, create awareness, report violations — lead by example. Remember, no one from above is coming to save us.

Lessons from Other Nations

Let's steal some ideas — the good ones — from countries that get civic sense right:

- **Singapore:** Stringent fines for littering, chewing gum, and even jaywalking keep the country spotless.

But it's more than fear — Singaporeans feel a collective pride in their clean streets.

- **Japan:** Children clean their classrooms, and people carry their trash home when bins aren't available. Respect for public space is ingrained from childhood.
- **Switzerland:** Waste is meticulously sorted and recycled. Citizens take ownership of their environment.
- **Bhutan:** The world's first carbon-negative country — their philosophy of *Gross National Happiness* promotes sustainability and community well-being.

Why not India? We're no less capable. Our people behave impeccably in places like the Delhi Metro — proof that we can follow rules when the environment supports them.

Conclusion: It Starts with You

We complain about dirty streets and chaotic traffic — but **we are the problem**. If we want smart cities, we need to become smart citizens first. Gandhi once said, *"Be the change you wish to see in the world."*

So, let's stop waiting for someone else to clean up our mess. Let's rise, rebel, and reclaim our civic sense. Our streets, our air, our rivers, our dignity — they all depend on **us**.

Are you ready to wake up and lead the change?

www.ingramcontent.com/pod-product-compliance
Lightning Source LLC
LaVergne TN
LVHW041534070526
838199LV00046B/1657